Adult Coloring Book

F*cking Relax Swear Word

Swear words Stress Relieving Patterns

Ricky Dickman

Copyright © 2016 Ricky Dickman
All rights reserved. No part of this book may be reproduced or transmitted in any form by any means, electronic or mechanical, including photocopying, scanning and recording, or by any information storage and retrieval system, without permission in writing from the publisher, except for the review for inclusion in a magazine, newspaper or broadcast

ISBN: 1530262410
ISBN-13: 978-1530262410

Son of a bitch

Manufactured by Amazon.ca
Bolton, ON